4

ANIMALS ATTACK!

Elephants

Kris Hirschmann

KIDHAVEN PRESS
An imprint of Thomson Gale, a part of The Thomson Corporation

THOMSON
———✳———™
GALE

Detroit • New York • San Francisco • San Diego • New Haven, Conn. • Waterville, Maine • London • Munich

© 2006 Thomson Gale, a part of The Thomson Corporation.

Thomson and Star Logo are trademarks and Gale and KidHaven Press are registered trademarks used herein under license.

For more information, contact
KidHaven Press
27500 Drake Rd.
Farmington Hills, MI 48331-3535
Or you can visit our Internet site at http://www.gale.com

LIBRARY OF CONGRESS CATALOGING-IN-PUBLICATION DATA

Hirschmann, Kris, 1967–
  Elephants / by Kris Hirschmann.
      p. cm. — (Animals attack!)
  Includes bibliographical references and index.
  ISBN 0-7377-3238-5 (hardcover : alk. paper)
  1. Elephants—Juvenile literature. 2. Animal attacks—Juvenile literature. I. Title.
II. Animals attack.
  QL737.P98H56 2005
  599.67—dc22
                                                                          2005008645

Printed in the United States of America

Contents

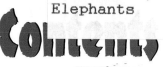

Chapter 1
Wild at Heart   4

Chapter 2
Danger in the Wild   14

Chapter 3
Captive Elephants on the Rampage   23

Chapter 4
The Deadliest Profession   32

Notes   41

Glossary   43

For Further Exploration   44

Index   46

Picture Credits   48

About the Author   48

Chapter 1

Wild at Heart

Most people have seen elephants in circuses, zoos, and amusement parks. Elephants often appear on television as well. In these situations, a person can see and marvel at an elephant's incredible size and power. Rarely does a person get to see an elephant using its power to defend itself. But elephant attacks do occur regularly, both in the wild and in **captivity**. Although no one keeps statistics about elephant attacks, it is likely that hundreds of people are killed by these animals every year.

Elephants attack for a number of reasons. They may become aggressive if people hurt them or just

Although this circus elephant seems gentle enough, she can be just as aggressive as elephants in the wild.

get too close. They may attack to assert their **dominance** or because they are in a bad mood. They may even attack to get revenge on people who have treated them badly in the past.

Getting Close to Elephants

The most dangerous elephants are the ones that roam freely in Africa and Asia. Wild elephants live in 37 African countries and 13 Asian countries—and in many places, these animals' ranges overlap with human farms and towns. It is very common for people who live in elephant areas to run into these

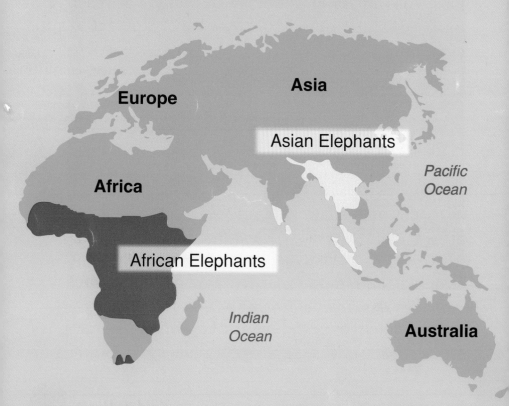

Where Wild Elephants Live

Europe

Asia

Asian Elephants

Pacific Ocean

Africa

African Elephants

Indian Ocean

Australia

creatures. Usually no harm is done during these encounters. But if something provokes an elephant to attack, people may be hurt or killed.

Another way humans encounter wild elephants is by going on **safaris**. Safaris allow thousands of people to have fun and safe elephant-watching experiences every year. Every now and then, however, a safari group accidentally upsets an elephant. When this happens, an attack may result.

Although wild elephants are responsible for most attacks on humans, captive elephants can be very dangerous as well. Captive elephants are especially common in some parts of Asia, where they are used as working animals. They are trained to push logs, carry heavy loads, and do many other jobs. Also in Asian countries, as well as in other countries around the world, elephants are kept in circuses and zoos. Captive elephants work and live side by side with people every day. More contact sometimes means that when elephants get upset, their trainers—and other people in the immediate area—are the first to be attacked.

A Dominant Beast

Elephant attacks occur mostly because elephants are naturally aggressive. Elephant society works on a system of dominance, which means that the strongest and most assertive elephants get their way. The dominance system works well when elephants attack other elephants. Both opponents are big and strong. The fighting elephants may bruise or scratch each other, but they probably will not do serious harm. When an elephant attacks a person, however, the situation is different. Even a small elephant can seriously hurt or kill a person.

Many people get hurt because they do not understand that elephants are naturally dominant creatures. In the wild, the creatures that live near elephants know this, and they have the sense to keep their distance. But this is not always true of humans. Some people purposely and foolishly invade an elephant's personal space. When they do, they may pay with their lives.

Bulls in Musth

In elephant society, adult males (called **bulls**) are the most dominant animals. This means that bull elephants are usually much more aggressive than females (called **cows**). This quality can make bulls deadly to humans who get too close.

Bull elephants are especially dangerous when they are in a condition called **musth**, which occurs during mating season. When a bull is in musth, certain glands in his head swell. The glands begin to ooze blackish fluid that drips down the bull's cheeks like oily tears. At the same time, **hormone** levels inside the bull's body rise sharply. The hormones change the bull's behavior. An elephant that is usually calm may become angry and aggressive when he is in musth. He is likely to attack any creature he sees.

Two adult male elephants, known as bulls, butt heads as they fight for dominance of the herd.

Most bulls go into musth once a year for six to eight weeks at a time. The maddened elephants are almost impossible to control during this period. For this reason, almost all circus, zoo, and working elephants are females. Yet cow elephants can also be unpredictable. Because any elephant can go from gentle to furious in the blink of an eye, no one who lives or works near elephants can ever be completely safe.

Many Weapons

Elephants have many physical features that make them dangerous. The elephant's most important feature is its size. African elephants may stand 12 feet (3.7m) high at the shoulder, and they can weigh more than 15,000 pounds (6,810kg). Asian elephants may reach 11 feet (3.4m) in height and weigh 11,000 pounds (5,000kg). These numbers mean that a big elephant is between 75 and 100 times heavier than an average person. Even a small push from such a big creature can be deadly to a human.

Elephants are also fast. Recent studies prove that Asian elephants can reach speeds of 15 miles (24km) per hour for short distances. African ele-

How Big Is an Elephant?

| 12 feet |
| 11 feet |
| 10 feet |
| 9 feet |
| 8 feet |
| 7 feet |
| 6 feet |
| 5 feet |
| 4 feet |
| 3 feet |
| 2 feet |
| 1 foot |

Girl	White Rhino	African Elephant
115 lbs	8,000 lbs	12,000 lbs

phants can run at least this fast and probably faster. In comparison, the fastest adult humans can run between 11 and 17 miles (18 and 27km) per hour. An elephant is therefore speedy enough to catch just about any person.

An elephant's 6-foot- (1.8-m-) long trunk is another potentially deadly feature. The trunk is strong enough to pick up a 450-pound (204-kg) load. It is finely controlled by about 150,000 muscle bundles, so the elephant can twist and turn its trunk any way it likes. An elephant can easily wrap its trunk around a person, then pound the person against the ground or even squeeze the life out of its victim. An elephant's trunk can also fling a person into a treetop or hit someone hard enough to break bones.

Most elephants have yet another weapon: their ivory **tusks**. The tusks are long, hard, and pointed. An elephant can use its tusks to pick up people and toss them through the air. It may also drive its tusks into a person's body, causing blood loss and damaging internal organs. A person who has been **gored** by an elephant may die if he or she does not get immediate medical help.

Safety Is Not Guaranteed

It is very hard to stop an elephant once it has decided to charge. For this reason, people who spend time near elephants do their best to avoid provoking these creatures. Villagers in elephant territory, for example, may stay indoors or climb trees when

A captive elephant in India bites down on the legs of its trainer and shakes him violently. The trainer died later from his injuries.

elephants approach. Safari guides make sure their groups maintain a safe distance from elephants. And zoo handlers, circus trainers, and other people who work with elephants every day use special techniques to establish their dominance over their charges. An elephant who accepts that its trainer is the boss is less likely to attack.

But elephants are wild animals, and they are unpredictable. No matter how careful a person is, he or she may still provoke an elephant to attack—and when this happens, injury or death may be the result. As long as people live near and work with elephants, tragedies will continue to occur.

Chapter 2

Danger in the Wild

Huge numbers of wild elephants roam the savannas of Africa and the jungles of Asia. The African elephant population is between 300,000 and 600,000. The Asian elephant population is between 35,000 and 50,000. These creatures are proud, strong, and dominant, and they believe the land belongs to them.

Unfortunately, people believe the same thing. Many humans feel entitled to live, walk, and hunt wherever they like—and this is when conflict occurs. When people get too close to wild elephants, attacks are likely to happen.

Protecting the Herd

People sometimes provoke an elephant attack by hurting a herd member. Elephants do not flee if a person harms a fellow elephant. They become angry and do their best to kill the person who is responsible.

As a world-famous ivory hunter in the late 1800s and early 1900s, Jim Sutherland knew this fact. It was Jim's job to shoot and kill elephants, so he was often charged by surviving herd members. Usually Jim managed to escape untouched from these encounters. But one day in 1908, his luck ran

Feeling threatened by the photographer, a female African elephant charges. People who approach elephants put themselves at risk for attack.

out. On this day Jim and his gunbearer, Simba, ran into a group of five bull elephants. Jim shot and killed four of the bulls. But a bad shot left the fifth elephant alive. The bull rushed at the hunter, screaming as it came. Jim shot the elephant in the left eye, but the enraged bull just kept coming.

In an instant, the furious elephant was upon Jim. The bull smashed Jim in the thigh, throwing him to the ground. The bull then picked up Jim and tossed him into the air. Jim landed on the bull's back, then bounced off and dropped to the ground, where he lay groaning between the elephant's feet. Jim thought he was about to die. "In which way is he going to kill me?" he wondered. "Will he kneel on and trample me horribly? Will he drive his tusk right through my body, or will he, by some heaven-sent chance, leave me alone? Whichever way it is, may it be swiftly over and done with!"[1]

But the elephant did not trample or gore Jim. Instead, he picked up Jim and tossed him into a nearby treetop. Badly hurt, Jim lost consciousness as he tumbled out of the tree. When he woke up, he saw the elephant standing about 90 feet (27m) away. Jim tried to get up and run, but his injuries were too severe. So he grabbed his gun and aimed. His first shot just irritated the elephant, which immediately began to charge once again. Jim waited . . . waited . . . waited . . . and when the elephant was about 40 feet (12m) away, Jim squeezed the trigger one final time. The bullet hit between the elephant's eyes, and the angry animal dropped dead at Jim's feet.

Built to Attack!

Elephants can stand up to 12 feet high and weigh more than 15,000 pounds.

Tusks can be used to gore its victims.

Six-foot-long trunk can lift up to 450 pounds.

Elephants can run fast—over 15 miles per hour for short distances.

Too Close for Comfort

The elephant that attacked Jim was fighting for its life. But sometimes elephants attack even when there is no threat. This was the case in 1999, when amateur photographer Stephen Street was on safari in Botswana. Stephen's sightseeing group was out walking one evening when a 6,000-pound (2,700-kg) cow burst from the bushes and headed straight for Stephen. Here is Stephen's account of what happened next.

"[The elephant] struck me (probably with her trunk), and I stumbled as I ran. Somehow I managed to avoid falling, regain my balance, and keep on running. She struck me again; falling to the floor I rolled and tumbled across the sand. I was lying face down when she hit me again, crushing me into the ground. I felt my bones break and my insides seemed to burst."[2]

Badly injured, Stephen waited for death. But it did not come. The group's guide shot and killed the elephant, stopping her deadly attack. Stephen was rushed to the hospital, where doctors discovered that he had two broken shoulders, six broken ribs, a broken leg, a punctured lung, and heavy internal bleeding. Stephen almost died from his injuries. But after nearly two weeks in intensive care, Stephen managed to survive his elephant encounter.

These tourists on safari in South Africa might feel safe in their vehicle, but this elephant is actually strong enough to overturn the car.

Walking unprotected through the bush, like Stephen did, is definitely the most dangerous way to see elephants. But visitors in vans and cars are not immune from elephant attacks. In one recent incident, a young bull overturned a South African tour bus and sent the ten passengers inside fleeing into the wilderness. And in South Africa's Hluhluwe-Imfolozi Park, elephants regularly kick and slap vehicles when tourists drive too close.

Living Together

Not all elephant/human encounters happen when people go looking for elephants. Sometimes elephants approach human villages instead. This is a problem in many parts of Africa and Asia, where wild elephants are being crowded into smaller and smaller areas by human population growth. When this happens, elephants become more likely to wander near people's homes and farms. They may encounter and attack their human neighbors.

Roaming elephants are a big problem in the Jharkhand area of India. Between 2000 and 2003, a herd of elephants killed 37 people and damaged 1,373 houses in a three-block area of the Dumka district. The herd first entered the village while trying to find a new migration route between summer and winter homes. It stayed because the food was good. "Once they have tasted banana, rice and haira [a beerlike brew], they come in search of more and kill whoever comes their way,"[3] explained a local forest officer.

A Ugandan man runs for his life as a group of angry bulls charges behind him.

To keep themselves safe, villagers flee to treetop shelters called machan whenever elephants approach. Some laboring women have even been forced to give birth to babies in their machan when elephants invaded. Villagers described these conditions in a petition to the Jharkhand High Court. "We have given birth to our babies under unimaginable conditions on machan. . . . We still are running for our lives with babies in arms, without any medical aid, leaving our homes at the mercy of the elephants."[4]

To control the wild elephants, government officials in 2005 hired two trained elephants and their handlers. The trained elephants drive wild elephants away from human homes and toward areas where they can be trapped. It remains to be seen whether this effort will make a difference in Dumka's elephant problem.

Staying Safe

The use of trained elephants is an unusual response to a desperate situation. More commonly, officials try to move dangerous herds to remote areas where they will not bother people. If this is not possible, herds may be **culled**. Culling is the government-approved killing of elephants. Depending on the situation, specific elephants may be targeted for death, or the killing of entire herds may be authorized. Professional hunters are hired to do the deadly job.

Individual farmers sometimes kill elephants as well. In most countries, however, it is against the law to shoot an elephant without government approval. So farmers use other methods to keep their property and their families safe from elephants. They may spray the edges of their land with pepper-scented liquid, which sometimes drives away elephants. They may also set off firecrackers to scare elephants or put up electric fences to keep them out. None of these methods can stop a really determined elephant, but they may help to keep less aggressive elephants at bay.

Safari groups also take steps to protect themselves from elephants. Guides try to maintain a safe distance from these creatures. Because elephants

Hired by the government of Zimbabwe to kill a herd of dangerous elephants, a team of hunters spots their prey.

have a keen sense of smell, guides also keep their groups downwind of any elephant herd. And in case both of these protections fail, guides carry powerful weapons at all times. If a safari group is charged, a guide can usually kill the attacking elephant before it hurts anyone.

Because safari guides are so well trained, tourists trust them with their lives. But guns can jam and bullets can miss their targets. People who go looking for elephants expect a thrilling adventure—but sometimes they get more than they bargained for. When elephants roam freely, danger is always right around the corner.

Chapter 3

Captive Elephants on the Rampage

Thousands of elephants are kept in captivity around the world. Most of the time, they are friendly and tame. But every now and then a captive elephant becomes enraged. It **rampages** out of control, hurting and sometimes killing innocent bystanders.

No one is sure why captive elephants rampage. Animal behavior experts point out, however, that captive elephants do not get the social contact and exercise that they enjoy in the wild. Living without these things may seem like a terrible punishment to an elephant. As a result, it is possible that captive elephants feel angry and resentful most of the time.

Any small annoyance may cause an already irritated elephant to attack.

Towering Fury

Sometimes elephants attack for a clear reason. For example, a person may do something that upsets an elephant. An attack of this nature happened in 2000 in Thailand. British tourist Geoffrey Taylor and his daughters, Helen and Andrea, were attending a performing-elephant show. According to some accounts, Andrea offered a bull elephant a banana, then pulled it away. Other witnesses say some tourists sitting behind Andrea held the banana. Everyone agrees that the elephant reached for food, only to have it snatched away. The elephant thought it was being teased, and it became enraged.

What happened next was sudden and horrifying. "[The elephant] suddenly lunged at the three of us," explained Geoffrey Taylor. "I did not see the moment the animal attacked as I had turned away. All I recall is being flung to the side. . . . There was total panic and blood everywhere."[5] The furious elephant jabbed the sisters with its tusks and tossed Andrea into the air.

All three family members were injured in the attack. Geoffrey suffered a gaping wound in his leg. Helen and Andrea were both gored in the stomach. The Taylors were rushed to a local hospital, where doctors fought to save their lives. Geoffrey and Helen were soon out of danger. Andrea's wounds,

A rampaging elephant can cause serious injuries with its enormous bulk and its sharp tusks.

however, were more serious. After three hours of surgery, Andrea died from her injuries.

Following this incident, a zoo warden in England commented on the Taylor family's experience. "All elephants are unpredictable, bull elephants especially," he said. "Allowing mature bull elephants into contact with people in an enclosed space is an accident waiting to happen."[6]

Angry Bulls

Dozens of incidents in the history of zoos and circuses prove the warden is right. Captive bulls are much more likely to rampage than captive cows. For this reason, bull elephants almost never appear in U.S. circuses today. They are sometimes kept in zoos as breeding animals, but they are considered much too dangerous to be in contact with the public.

In many foreign countries, however, bull elephants are still common in public areas. Sometimes

A captive bull in India throws his trainer from his back. Captive bulls are much more likely to attack than captive cows.

these "tame" bulls become angry and hurt the people near them. In February 2000, for example, a working bull in Thailand went into a frenzy for no apparent reason and crushed the arm of a nearby man. The man's arm was so badly injured that it had to be cut off. Just a week later in another part of Thailand, a bull elephant threw his handler off his back and went **berserk** in downtown Bangkok. The bull rampaged through the busy city streets as shoppers scattered, screaming. Police officers with tranquilizer guns managed to bring down the beast before anybody got hurt.

Gone Berserk

There is no doubt that most cow elephants are calmer and more even-tempered than bulls. But elephants, like people, have individual personalities. Certain cow elephants can be just as unpredictable as bulls. There have been many reports of cows going berserk and attacking people.

One widely reported incident occurred in 1992. A cow named Janet was performing at a circus in Florida. A mother and her five children were riding on Janet's back when the elephant suddenly became furious. Janet threw her trainer to the ground and tried to pull down the circus tent. Then she ran from the tent with her screaming passengers still on her back. Outside, Janet knocked down a police officer and just kept going. A circus worker hopped onto another elephant and chased Janet, soon pulling the terrified mother and her children to

A police officer outside Bangkok, Thailand, keeps a safe distance as he calls for backup to help subdue a rampaging elephant.

safety. Police officers then opened fire on Janet. It took 57 shots to bring down the enraged beast.

Two years later, a circus cow named Tyke went on a rampage in Hawaii. Just before going on stage, Tyke knocked down her trainer and killed him by stepping on his head. Then the elephant entered the arena, where she continued her attack. "All of a sudden, the elephant kicked [a worker] into the arena," a shaken spectator said later. When the worker was down on the ground, Tyke pummeled him with her feet, trunk, and head. "People started running away," said the spectator. "Children were screaming and we saw the blood."[7] A dozen people were injured as the crowd fled from the furious elephant. Meanwhile, Tyke abandoned her attack on the worker and broke out of the tent. Authorities chased Tyke for several blocks before cornering her on a quiet street. They had to shoot Tyke more than 100 times before she finally lay still.

Public Safety

Stories like these have convinced many people that no elephant can be trusted. Even some professional elephant workers feel this way. "My experience with the circus has convinced me that . . . elephants are extremely dangerous and should not be around the public. It never ceased to amaze me that the circus would tell people to put their children on an elephant's back when they knew how dangerous the elephant was,"[8] said former circus employee Tom Rider in a statement before the U.S. House of Representatives in 2000.

Some governments and organizations agree with Rider's view. In India, for example, elephants are not allowed to perform in circuses because of the danger to the public. And in the United States, the Association of Zoos and Aquariums has asked its members not to offer elephant rides due to safety concerns.

But many organizations ignore this request. They think that elephants are safe if handled properly. "People have ridden elephants for more than 5,000 years—almost as long as people have ridden horses," points out David Blasko, supervisor of elephant training at Six Flags Marine World in California. "The number of accidents or injuries to the public or to the elephants involved in elephant rides in the United States is exceedingly small."[9]

It is true that zoo and circus attendees are very unlikely to be attacked by elephants. But it does happen from time to time—and when it does, only luck can save the attack-victims' lives. An out-of-control elephant is too strong to be restrained, and it is too big to be brought down quickly by tran-

Animal-control officials in Manila, Philippines, try to move an escaped circus elephant that they brought down with tranquilizers.

A mother and child ride an elephant at a zoo in Miami. Their lives could be in danger should the elephant decide to attack.

quilizer guns. So until it is shot and killed, a rampaging elephant will do all the damage it wants. There is no escaping the fact that visitors who get close to captive elephants are making a small, but possibly deadly, gamble with their lives.

Chapter 4

The Deadliest Profession

Working with elephants is very dangerous. Between 600 and 700 professional elephant handlers work in the United States. On average, one of these people is killed by an elephant every year. Statistically, this makes elephant handling one of the nation's deadliest professions.

Experts believe elephants attack their handlers for two main reasons. In some cases, an elephant is simply trying to assert its dominance. In other cases, an elephant may be seeking revenge for past mistreatment.

Who Is in Charge?

In the elephant/trainer relationship, the trainer is the boss. Elephants are taught to respect the boss as stronger and more powerful than they are. As long as an elephant believes this is true, it will behave itself. But sometimes an elephant sees a weakness in its trainer. When this happens, the elephant may attack in an effort to become the new boss.

This may have been the reason for a fatal elephant attack at the London Zoo in 2002. A keeper named Jim Robson was running a show in which

The aggressive nature of elephants makes elephant handling one of the most dangerous professions in the world.

three cow elephants were moving logs around their pen. Suddenly Mya, who was usually the gentlest elephant, wrapped her trunk around Jim's legs and threw him to the ground. Mya held Jim down, then stamped on his head. Jim was rescued and taken to the hospital, but doctors were unable to save his life. He died two hours later from massive head injuries.

Zoo officials were astounded by Mya's violent act. Jim had been working with Mya since she was a baby. He trusted the elephant, and she was usually affectionate toward her trainer. It seemed unbelievable that Mya had turned vicious. But another trainer thought he might know why Mya had acted as she did. "[Jim] was confident around the elephants, but he didn't have the control I had," said Brian Harman, the zoo's head keeper. "I tend to be more assertive."[10] The zoo was having a staff shortage, so Jim was working alone. According to Harman, Mya may have sensed Jim's weakness and seized her chance to attack.

New Kid on the Block

The need for dominance may have caused the injury of elephant trainer Michael Embury as well. Michael began working at the MetroZoo in Miami, Florida, in October 2002. In December of that year, Michael and another trainer were giving a public presentation about elephant care and feeding when disaster struck. A 20-year-old cow named

Flora charged Michael without warning and threw him to the ground. Then she kicked him, sending him flying more than 15 feet (4.6m) into a pile of boulders.

Zoo officials quickly rescued Michael and rushed him to the hospital. Upon examination, doctors discovered that Michael had two broken shoulders, a broken arm, a damaged spleen, and a brain concussion. Michael had to spend nearly a month in the hospital, but he eventually recovered from his elephant encounter.

No one is sure why Flora attacked Michael. But zoo officials believe Michael's inexperience may have been a factor. "It's not terribly uncommon for elephants in a herd to sometimes challenge the new kid on the block," said MetroZoo spokesman Ron

A handler at a zoo in the Ukraine works with a newly arrived female to help her adjust to her new environment.

An Indian handler rides on the back of an elephant with his bull hook within reach.

Magill after the incident. "When [Flora is] testing another elephant, it's nothing but a little pushing and shoving. But when a 6,000-pound (2,724-kg) animal does that to a 175-pound (80-kg) man, it's a little different."[11]

Out for Revenge

While some elephants attack to show their dominance, others may be out for revenge. People who believe in the revenge theory say that elephants have very good memories. They never forget a cruel action, and they hold grudges against anyone who treats them badly. Bad treatment, unfortunately, was once a part of every elephant/trainer relationship. Elephant handlers beat their charges, stabbed them with sharp sticks called **bull hooks**, and burned them with blowtorches. They thought that the only way to control an elephant was through fear and intimidation.

Today, traditional elephant-training methods are illegal in many countries, including the United States. But industry insiders say that many elephants are still abused in secret. When abused elephants run out of patience, they may attack their trainers.

A bull elephant named Tamba may have been out for revenge in 1991. Tamba lived at the Metro Washington Park Zoo in Portland, Oregon. One day Tamba slammed his trainer against the wall. The trainer was hurt, but not badly. He decided that Tamba's actions were accidental, and he continued

A zookeeper in Tennessee gives an elephant a bath. The zoo allows its keepers to interact with elephants without the protection of safety barriers.

to work with the elephant. Seven months after the first incident, however, Tamba knocked the same trainer to the floor. This time the man's skull was fractured. Tamba's trainer survived the attack, but zoo officials decided it would be best to keep him away from Tamba from then on.

Job Security

The elephant industry may not be perfect, but conditions for captive elephants are much better than they used to be. Today most elephant trainers use affection and rewards, not fear and pain, as teaching tools. These positive training methods create a much better relationship between elephants and their keepers. And when elephants are happy, they are much less likely to attack.

But even the happiest elephant can turn deadly. For this reason, many zoos are changing the way their keepers interact with elephants. About half of all U.S. zoos have switched from **free contact** programs, where keepers mingle with elephants, to **protected contact** programs, where keepers manage and care for elephants through safety barriers. Protected contact is much safer for the humans who work with elephants every day. Yet many zoos continue their free-contact programs for various reasons. "We choose to do free contact because we believe it allows us to give better and superior care to the animals,"[12] says Paul Grayson of the Indianapolis Zoo, giving one common reason. Nearly all circuses, too, allow free contact between trainers and elephants. But this is not a matter of choice. Because of the way they travel and operate, very few circuses have the resources they would need to keep their workers and elephants separated.

People who interact with elephants know that their job is dangerous. Many choose to take the risk, however, because they love their work. "It's

For safety reasons, these elephant keepers at a Michigan zoo interact with their charges from behind a steel-cabled fence.

very hard to get out of the elephant business. I can't *imagine* being out of it,"[13] says one longtime elephant handler. This person and others do the best they can to stay safe each day. But every now and then, one of these trainers will make a small but critical error in judgment. An elephant will turn vicious—or perhaps it will just get too close. As one trainer points out, "You gotta remember that an elephant just leaning on you in love leaves nothing but a grease spot."[14] As long as elephants and humans live and work together, newspapers will carry stories about the tragedies that happen when elephants attack.

Notes

Chapter 2: Danger in the Wild

1. Quoted in Peter Hathaway Capstick, *The African Adventurers: A Return to the Silent Places.* New York: St. Martin's, 1992, p. 197.

2. Stephen Street, "Surviving the Charge," www.naturephotographers.net/ss01021.html.

3. Quoted in Kanhaiah Bhelari, "Tree-Top Babies," *The Week*, December 7, 2002. www.theweek.com/23dec07/life11.htm.

4. Quoted in Pranava K. Chaudhary, "Tribals Face Death Threat by Tuskers," *Asia Africa Intelligence Wire*, March 18, 2003. http://infotrac.galegroup.com.

Chapter 3: Captive Elephants on the Rampage

5. Quoted in Alex Spillius and Nigel Bunyan, "The Elephant Suddenly Lunged at Us," *Electronic Telegraph*, April 26, 2000. www.telegraph.co.uk.

6. Quoted in Nigel Bunyan, "Death of Briton Gored by Elephant Still a Mystery," *Electronic Telegraph*, May 12, 2000. www.telegraph.co.uk.

7. Quoted in Associated Press, "My Son Doesn't Ever Want to Go Back to the Circus," *St.*

Petersburg Times, August 22, 1994. http://pqasb.pqarchiver.com/sptimes.

8. Tom Rider, hearing before the U.S. House of Representatives, transcript, June 13, 2000. http://commdocs.house.gov/committees/judi ciary/hju65825.000/hju65825_0.htm.

9. David Blasko, hearing before the U.S. House of Representatives, transcript, June 13, 2000.

Chapter 4: The Deadliest Profession

10. Quoted in Helen Rumbelow, "Gentlest Elephant Killed Her Zoo Keeper," reprinted from TimesOnline.com, March 12, 2002. www. plumed-serpent.com/elephant.html.

11. Quoted in Anita Srikameswaran, "Zoo Here Offers Aid, Sympathy After Miami Elephant Attack," *Pittsburgh Post-Gazette*, December 17, 2002. www.post-gazette.com/localnews/2002 1217elephantreg3p3.asp.

12. Quoted in Don Hopey, "Elephant Attacks on Humans Rare, Unexplained, Unpredictable," *Pittsburgh Post-Gazette*, November 19, 2002. www.post-gazette.com/healthscience/20021119 elephants1119p3.asp.

13. Quoted in Shana Alexander, *The Astonishing Elephant*. New York: Random House, 2000, p. 31.

14. Quoted in Alexander, *The Astonishing Elephant*, p. 33.

Glossary

berserk: Uncontrollable and crazed.

bull hooks: Rods with a sharp, curved metal prong on one end. Some trainers use bull hooks to control elephants.

bulls: Adult male elephants.

captivity: Living confined and cared for by human beings rather than living freely in the wild.

cows: Adult female elephants.

culled: To make an elephant population smaller by killing selected members or a preset number of individuals.

dominance: Strength, aggressiveness, and the ability to be in control.

free contact: Programs in which trainers mingle freely with elephants.

gored: Stabbed by an elephant's tusk.

hormone: Substance made by the body to carry chemical messages through the blood stream. Hormones have a strong effect on an animal's behavior.

musth: A state that bull elephants enter when they are ready to mate. Bulls in musth are often angry, aggressive, and unpredictable.

protected contact: Programs in which trainers care for elephants through safety barriers.

rampages: Rushes about wildly and uncontrollably.

safaris: Trips, usually to Africa, made for the purpose of seeing, photographing, or hunting wild animals.

tusks: Enlarged, pointed teeth that stick out of an elephant's mouth. An elephant may use its tusks as weapons.

For Further Exploration

Books

Kathy Darling, *The Elephant Hospital.* Brookfield, CT: Millbrook, 2000. Describes the work of the Friends of the Asian Elephant's Elephant Hospital in Thailand. This unique organization treats sick, injured, and mistreated Asian elephants.

S.K. Eltringham, *The Illustrated Encyclopedia of Elephants.* London: Smithmark, 1997. This reference book is a complete guide to every aspect of elephant life.

Judith Presnall, *Animals with Jobs: Circus Animals.* San Diego: KidHaven, 2002. Read about the daily lives of circus elephants, plus lions, tigers, horses, and other circus animals.

Ian Redmond, *Eyewitness: Elephant.* New York: DK, 2000. This fact-filled book about elephants is packed with incredible photographs.

Bonnie Worth, *Jumbo: The Most Famous Elephant in the World!* New York: Random House, 2001. This book tells the sometimes sad but always fascinating true story of Jumbo the elephant, the former star of Barnum & Bailey's "Greatest Show on Earth."

Web Sites

Animal Bytes: Elephant (www.sandiegozoo. org/animalbytes/t-elephant.html). This site has lots of good basic information about African and Asian elephants. Visitors can click on the links to listen to a recording of an African elephant or "adopt" an elephant of their very own.

The EleCam (www.tappedintoelephants.com/ asp/index.php). This site broadcasts live images from The Elephant Sanctuary in Hohenwald, Tennessee. Be patient and you may see real elephants in action.

The Plight of Elephants in Circuses (www. petaliterature.com/ENT248.pdf). Published by People for the Ethical Treatment of Animals, this booklet discusses the negative aspects of keeping elephants in captivity.

Index

African elephants, 10–11, 14
Asian elephants, 7, 10, 14
Association of Zoos and
  Aquariums, 29
attacks
  dominance system and, 32,
    33–35, 37
  preventing, 11, 13, 20–22,
    29–31
  reasons for, 4, 6–7, 15–16,
    19–20, 24
  without reason, 17–19,
    27–29, 39

Blasko, David, 30
bull hooks, 37
bulls, 8–9, 26–27, 37–38

captive elephants
  bulls as, 26–27
  cows as, 9
  culling and, 21
  jobs of, 7
  rampages by, 23–24, 27–29
  training methods used on,
    37–39

circuses, 7
  attacks in, 27–29, 39
  bulls in, 26
  cows in, 9
  dominance system in, 13
contact programs, 39
cows
  aggressiveness of, 8
  attacks by, 27–29, 34–35,
    37
  unpredictability of, 9
culling, 21

deaths, 4, 32
dominance, system of, 7–8,
  13, 32, 33–35

Embury, Michael, 34–35, 37

Flora (cow), 35, 37
free contact programs, 39

Grayson, Paul, 39

handlers
  abuse by, 37–38

dominance system and, 32, 33–35
Harman, Brian, 34
Hawaii, 28–29
herds, 15–16, 21
Hluhluwe-Imfolozi Park (South Africa), 19
hormones, 8
human development, 19–20

India, 19, 29

Janet (cow), 27–28
Jharkhand area (India), 19

London Zoo, 33–34

machans, 20
Magill, Ron, 35, 37
mating season, 8–9
Metro Washington Park Zoo (Portland, Oregon), 37–38
MetroZoo (Miami, Florida), 34–35, 37
musth, 8–9
Mya (cow), 34

personalities, 7–8, 26–29
population, 14
public safety, 29–31

rampages, 23–24, 27–29
range, 6–7
revenge, 32, 37–38

Rider, Tom, 29
Robson, Jim, 33–34

safaris
  attacks on, 17–18
  preventing attacks on, 13, 21–22
  safety of, 7
Simba (gunbearer), 16
size, 10
smell, sense of, 22
South Africa, 19
speed, 10–11
Street, Stephen, 17–18
Sutherland, Jim, 15–16

Tamba (bull), 37–38
Taylor, Andrea, 24–25
Taylor, Geoffrey, 24–25
Taylor, Helen, 24–25
Thailand, 24–25
training methods, 37–39
tusks, 11
Tyke (cow), 28–29

weapons, 10–11
working elephants, 7

zoos, 7
  attacks in, 33–35, 37–38
  bulls in, 26
  contact programs in, 39
  cows in, 9
  dominance system in, 13

Picture Credits

About the Author

Kris Hirschmann has written more than 100 books for children. She is the president of The Wordshop, a business that provides a variety of writing and editorial services. She holds a bachelor's degree in psychology from Dartmouth College in Hanover, New Hampshire.

Hirschmann lives just outside Orlando, Florida, with her husband Michael and her daughters Nikki and Erika.